Many Millions Strong

Your Victory Guide to a Bernie Sanders Landslide

Stan Munslow

4G Publishing

The author would like to thank BrainyQuote.com for the many profound and stirring quotations used in this book. Like Bernie Sanders, *Brainy Quote* helps bring a higher level of thinking to the world.

"Deep into that darkness peering, long I stood there, wondering, fearing, doubting, dreaming dreams no mortal ever dared to dream before."

Edgar Allan Poe

Dedication

For America: the people, the land, the promise.

Table of Contents

INTRODUCTION

Your Call to Action

*"Never doubt that a small group of thoughtful,
committed citizens can change the world; indeed,
it's the only thing that ever has."*
Margaret Mead, used with permission

A Year Brimming With Promise

Are you still in shock? Are you still in awe? Has it started to sink in yet?

Fellow impassioned Americans, how long has it been? How long have we been waiting for a moment like this? Just think! We, the American People – "The 99%" – have just been blessed with the opportunity to elect a president like no other; a leader poised to return America to its citizens. Indeed, Senator Bernie Sanders is not only the *best* candidate we've had in a woefully long time, he is, quite frankly, a *revolutionary figure* in the greatest sense of the term. Bernie Sanders is a man *so* full of integrity, *so* qualified to lead, *so* fit for the job of president, and *so* in-tune with the needs, pains, and yearnings of the average citizen, it makes the head spin in amazement and the imagination soar at the very wonder of it all.

The wonder and the dream of *what could be.*

The truth of the matter is that Bernie Sanders is more in-touch with what we want and what is best for America than even we ourselves are. If there is one thing this man has come to learn during his half-century of listening to, empathizing with, and fighting for the American people it is, quite simply, *us.*

Bernie Sanders has learned *us.* Bernie Sanders *knows* us. Bernie Sanders *is* us.

And now, for the first time in many a year, we have the opportunity to elect a president whose every lofty idea, every well-thought-out plan, and every sincere promise for America is actually borne of and based upon the radical notion that a United States president *should* do what is right for *We the People*, not for whichever corporate donors have paid the most for his or her election and who, when the time comes to pay the piper, are going to want a hefty return on their investment.

Just imagine a president *not* beholden to the big banks.

Imagine a president acting on behalf of working Americans first, corporate America second (or perhaps third).

Imagine a president who *truly* wants Americans to enjoy some of the advantages enjoyed by people in those (often Scandinavian) countries which, all too often, put us to shame with their statistically high degree of happiness, their laudable level of personal prosperity, and their downright enviable quality of life.

Advantages such as:

- A minimum wage that *doesn't* result in a life of poverty for those willing and able to work forty hours a week

- Free and debt-free public colleges and universities to help us become the best-educated nation on Earth

- Free childcare and pre-k programs: ideas that represent *real* family values … for a change

- A single-payer universal healthcare system that would put America on par with most other developed nations where health and wellness is considered to be a fundamental human right, not a commodity

- Roads, bridges, airports, dams, and rail systems that are once again safe, reliable, and the envy of the world

And, when it comes to our precious and irreplaceable environment, just imagine a president who will actually say no to those corporations who, until now, have refused to clean up their own messes and who have been allowed to treat our land, our air, and our water – indeed our entire ecosystem – as theirs for the ravaging.

Of course – as your finger-wagging Republican friends are likely to "inform" you – most of these programs would be paid for with (Egad!) tax dollars. (The horror of it all!) To which you might wish to respond: "Yes, but since we already pay taxes anyway, which would *you* prefer to see that money go toward? Big bank bailouts, offshore corporate tax havens, and unending wars of aggression … or *your* medical care, college for *your* children, conscientious care for *our* veterans, and the upkeep of *our* roads and bridges? This tax money is *our* money! We have a say in where it goes and who it helps! Wouldn't you prefer that it go toward programs that improve *our* quality of life, rather than yet another corporate handout?"

These are just a few of the advantages that Bernie Sanders wants for America because – and this is important – if we are, in fact, living in the greatest nation on Earth, then shouldn't every American have the opportunity to enjoy the greatest quality of life on Earth?

These are advantages that Bernie Sanders wants for us because, in the end, it is the *right thing to do.*

Imagine an America with this kind of leader in the Oval Office.

Indeed, how lucky we are!

There's just this one small detail:

Bernie Sanders needs to get elected.

Of course, his poll numbers are getting better all the time. Yes, the attendance at his rallies – often in the tens of thousands – puts every other candidate to shame. Yes, his supporters are second to none in their level of devotion. Nonetheless, two important concerns remain:

One: *We need an insurance policy.* We need to make absolutely certain that Bernie Sanders gets in the White House because otherwise this incredible opportunity is gone. And, as you are likely well aware: *It's Bernie or nothing.* Who else is going to come along with his degree of integrity, his amount of experience in public office, or his level of commitment to put the American people first? *Who?* Perhaps someone would come along – someday – perhaps even someone who is actually electable. But are you willing to bet your quality of life and your future on such an unlikelihood as that?

No! This is too important to risk losing. There is far too much at stake. And make no mistake: If *any* other candidate gets in, it will be all over. Big money and big business will then have at least four more years during which to grow even bolder, even more audacious, more demanding, and more powerful. They will have even more control over our government and our lives.

Then you can just kiss those nascent dreams of yours goodbye.

Indeed, it's Bernie Sanders ... or nothing.

Two: *the corporate news media.* Thanks to their near complete dismissal of the nationwide Bernie Sanders phenomenon, it is plain to see they are banking on the hope that if they just keep ignoring him, downplaying him, and marginalizing him, he will just go away and make their billionaire owners and advertisers very happy.

No, they are not going to make it easy for Bernie Sanders. Or us.

Well, here's a news flash for any members of corporate news media who seek to continue to misinform their viewers: You may have the lights, the cameras, and the well-costumed pundits, but we have something better:

We, those who support Bernie Sanders and who understand that he is the only real choice America has, are *many millions strong*! And that beats bright, colorful studios and a herd of on-air talent any day. Why? Because each and every one of us can vote!

Many Millions Strong

Yes, we, the many millions strong, have within our very number the strength, conviction, certainty, and power to override the corporate news media's Bernie Sanders blackout. Through our vote we have the power to say no to the 1%. Indeed, we have almost unimaginable power; we have passion, and we have unstoppable desire. We are many millions strong and we are growing ever more fed up and fired up because, for the first time in very nearly *ever*, we have been given a reason to dream; a chance to dream big.

And we are *not* going to let those dreams be taken away again.

Read those words once more: *many millions strong*. Breathe them in. Let them empower and embolden you with their energy. They are so powerful. You *can* do this. We *can* do this. We have the power to steer the United States away from its destiny of absolute corporate totalitarianism. We have this power, but only if we *say* we do.

We have this power if we simply act upon our dreams with the same conviction and "take no prisoners" confidence of …

Donald Trump.

Yes, *that* Donald Trump. His is perhaps the last name you would expect to see, or hope to see, in this book. But just watch this man. Seriously, watch him. Delusional or not, mean-spirited or not, buffoon or not, it is astounding to see him in action. No matter what the issue, even an issue he knows nothing about or has no background in, he speaks of it as if he is God's gift to the entirety of human knowledge and wisdom. It goes without saying that many people believe in him, not because of his political capabilities (whatever they may be), or because his words seem to convey some enticing semblance of credibility or brilliance, but *solely because* he believes in himself to such an over-the-top degree. His belief in himself, warranted or not, is infallible to the nth degree. And it is from here that men like him garner much of their success.

When it comes to the rabble-rousing power of belief, we can all learn something from this man.

Belief is, in fact, *so* powerful that it is not only astounding, it is *everything*. Consider all those Olympic gold medalists who cite their unshakable belief in themselves as a primary source of power behind their victories and world records. Consider the many terminal cancer patients who, after being told by their doctors to go home and die, spontaneously rid their bodies of all traces of their disease. Consider the fact that, standing behind virtually every success story on the planet is a firm, abiding belief in oneself, one's abilities, and the very outcome one seeks.

Belief is not just a game-changer. To a very large extent ... it *is* the game.

Now, you take that belief – in this case, your belief in Bernie Sanders and what a man like him can do for America – you get it white-hot with conviction and desire, then you let it course through every cell in your body.

Then ... you *multiply* it.

You multiply it by millions. Again, we are many millions strong. Don't believe even for one second that those banks and corporations have a power equal to ours. They simply do not. They are, at best, a few thousand strong. We are stronger by a thousand fold. And don't think that the heads of those banks and corporations don't know this. Somewhere in the back of their minds lurks the fear that if, one day, millions of people were to rise in unison and declare "Enough!" their game would be all over.

Because, in the end, how can anyone or anything possibly stand up to millions of people, people who are informed, angry, energized, and bound by the same convictions?

One more time: We are many millions strong! And we have determination, we have passion, and we have unwavering belief – both in Bernie Sanders as well as in our ability to get him on the ballot and into the White House.

So if it is true, as Margaret Mead said that a small group of thoughtful, committed citizens can, in fact, change the world … just think – *think* – what we, many-millions-strong as we are, can do!

We Need Champions

Alas, the 1%, the big banks, the transnationals, and the corporate news media conglomerates are going to put up the fight of their lives by grooming candidates who are willing to bend to their every whim, then bankrolling their campaigns with so much cash you can smell it from here.

Therefore, until Election Day 2016, *please* make helping Bernie Sanders to get elected your new side job. Please utilize as much of your disposable time as possible doing all that is in your power to make certain that Bernie Sanders wins the presidency.

Many will argue that they don't have the time. Oh, yes, you do. Every one of us has the same twenty-four hours a day that Helen Keller had. We have the same twenty-four hours as Michael Jordan, Bill Gates, or Bernie Sanders. So if you can't find the time, then *make* the time. Make time for this by prioritizing it above lesser activities. You will do this if it is important to you. If saving your Social Security, saving our planet, and saving our great country from corporate takeover are important to you, rest assured: You *will* find a way.

You see, this is, in fact, more than your new job; much more. This is big. And if Bernie is to win, and win big, then we, his supporters, need to think and act like champions. We need to embark upon this journey in the way of an athlete seeking gold at the Olympics, or an entrepreneur endeavoring to make millions. By going all-out, full-tilt, and all the way in every way. By investing ourselves completely in this endeavor. Through work, sweat, and sacrifice. Through time, money, and effort. Whatever it takes, that's what we do; that's what champions do.

As the great motivator, Anthony Robbins puts it: "Success is massive determined action."

Action is the buzzword of champions. They take massive determined action every day – and the "massive" part is not lost on them. They pour every ounce of themselves into their quest. They give it everything they have. And, far from getting "tired" from all that effort, they find themselves *energized* by it. It fuels them. It exhilarates them. It empowers them and propels them to even greater effort and greater success.

That is what this book is calling upon you to do. You, along with your many millions of Bernie Sanders election teammates, are going to *go for it* like you've never gone for anything before. No wimping out, no cashing in. And no regrets later on, thinking that you could have done more.

And do you want to know why? Do you want to know why in God's name you or anyone else would choose to put themselves through the rigor of going all out in their efforts to help Bernie Sanders become our next president?

Because consider the alternatives:

Consider a Donald Trump administration. Think about what that would be like. Think about what that would *mean* – to you, to America, and to our relationship with the international community.

Reflect upon a Ben Carson reign. What would *that* be like? It boggles the mind to visualize our amazing country suddenly being so woefully "misled."

Or, we could settle for Hillary. In cahoots as ever with Wall Street. More power to the corporations. More, more, and more funding for the machines of war. And, at the very least, business as usual. Business as usual *ad infinitum*.

Either way, there go your dreams. There goes the promise of an honest, wise, effective leader in the White House. Someone who truly can make this country a place you would want to live your life in, as it was decades ago, as it was before the 1% became the 1% and began heedlessly lowering the quality of life for everyone else in their mad quest to join the ranks of the 1%.

There goes the chance of having a President who would serve the needs of the American People. Instead, yet another who, to some degree or other, marginalizes and exploits the 99% for the whims and wants of the 1% who, themselves, have moved so far into the realm of audacity and greed and self-aggrandizement that it leaves one wondering if these men and women are men and women at all and not some lesser, baser version of the terms.

So, like the Olympian who has gold in his or her eyes, you – along with the rest of us – embark upon this journey to bring Bernie Sanders to the White House with all the energy you can muster, all the effort you can give, and all the conviction you can generate – the conviction that this truly is the greatest opportunity we've had in many, many years – one that *cannot* be squandered with anything less than one hundred percent on our part.

One final point:

You aren't just doing this in order to convert potential Hillary Clinton voters, potential GOP voters, and potential non-voters into Bernie Sanders voters. You are there to inspire *other Bernie Sanders supporters* into doing more to help spread the Bernie Sanders message – so that they, too, will be inspired to help light up others within *their* circles, within *their* locales, and within *their* spheres of influence.

Do you see where this is going? It's called *wildfire*! Everyone reading this book tells everyone they know about Bernie. Everyone reading this book tells everyone they know *to tell everyone they know about Bernie.* You are not just recruiting Bernie supporters. You are recruiting Bernie-supporter *recruiters*!

Wildfire.

Are you on fire over Bernie Sanders yet? Are you feeling the Bern?

Then let us begin doing all that we can to become a part of history and elect our next great President.

PART ONE

WE CAN MAKE IT HAPPEN

"Vision without action is merely a dream. Action without vision just passes the time. Vision with action can change the world."

Joel A. Barker

Stan Munslow

CHAPTER ONE

Get Ready, Get Psyched, Win!

*To accomplish great things we must first dream,
then visualize, then plan ... believe ... act!*
Alfred A. Montapert

When was the last time so many people dared to dream, in unison, the same great and lofty dream? How long has it been? For how many years have Americans stood by and watched the 1% – the billionaires and their kind – being granted demand after audacious demand, privilege after inequitable privilege? For how many years have we stood back and watched them bend and shape our government into a tool with which to realize their own goals and dreams, often at the expense of, and always indifferent to, our own?

At first, the great powers, holding back their backroom chortling, told us to be patient, to work harder, and that soon a part of the wealth would begin to just "trickle down" to everyone.

It all sounded so credible, so alluring. So we bought the baloney – that baloney which, of course, turned out to be *so* absurd that, to this day, we continue to kick ourselves for having bought it. And, as those years went by and the trickling never came, the ceaseless promises of "trickle down" began to diminish. So demoralized we were becoming, so accustomed to our lot, that there was simply no further need, neither by government nor corporate America, to keep pushing that Kool-Aid on us in order to keep us docile and quiet. We were sufficiently stifled, broken even.

No, no further need to keep that promise out in public view ... where it just might get scrutinized a little too closely and subsequently exposed for the pile of bullshit that it is. Better to just mention it occasionally, leaving it as a quiet murmur in the backdrop of our increasingly less fulfilling lives in order to make damned sure we stayed quiet.

So there we remained, in a sort of fitful slumber. Working, working, and working some more. Finding it increasingly impossible to pay for necessities on two forty-hour-week paychecks, let alone "extravagances" such as medical coverage and college tuition. Finding it increasingly necessary to add on a few more work hours here and shave off a few more vacation days there. Doing more. Getting less. Doing still more. Getting still less (except for, perhaps, a shiny new technology toy every so often with which to keep ourselves distracted and even more docile). And all the while working for inadequate wages so that the 1% could have everything they need in order to realize their own ever-upward-spiraling dreams while our own dreams ... well, who has time to dream anymore anyway?

We were just beginning to sense that the only "trickling" going on in this country was of the *"trickle up"* kind.

Then some guy from Vermont had to come along and start shaking everyone from their oblivion. Suddenly, we began to hear a voice – a wise, compassionate, and shockingly trustworthy voice – begin to rise up over that din of "trickle-down" nonsense. And that voice was saying "Hey, wake up, everybody! Wake up and start dreaming again!"

And there went the sanctity of our increasingly uncomfortable comfort zone – the well-worn familiarity of our ever-shrinking same-old.

Suddenly, there was Senator Bernie Sanders, I-Vermont, showing up all over the country and across the Internet, telling us of how things could be, how citizen-friendly life already was in other countries, and how he could help us have some of that citizen-friendly life ourselves.

He told us about unheard-of notions like "universal healthcare" and "free public college." He told us about reigning in the Wall Street speculators and the corporate tax dodgers. He told us about a federal minimum wage that a single mom could actually live on and about fixing our increasingly embarrassing and dangerous roads, bridges, and rail systems.

It all sounded so … *nice*. Intoxicating even. But then, as we began to awaken further, we thought about it a little. "Hey, wait a minute," people started saying. "What do you think this is?

Norway or something? America doesn't do 'feel good' stuff like that anymore. At least not for the 99%. After all, how would we afford it?"

So he went on to explain that the money for such luxuries as beating cancer without bankruptcy was, in fact, already there. It had just been temporarily misappropriated to the whims and the demands of the 1% – to the bank bailouts, the offshore tax havens, and the military tools with which to fight endless wars on countless shores. We *could*, in fact, afford these things and even help the economy at the same time.

And that was that. There was no stopping those dreams from stirring us wide awake now. And we've been dreaming ever since. And growing restless. And getting excited.

And feeling the Bern.

We want Bernie Sanders in the White House, damn it! We have HAD IT with the 1% getting more and more and *We the People* – the people that actually comprise this nation and make it run – getting less and less … and still less. We want back the life that average, hard-working Americans enjoyed years ago – those bucolic post-war years on through the seventies that had been so … livable – up until 1980, when America embarrassed itself in the eyes of the world by electing as their president a Hollywood actor who, in his Hollywood-trained voice of oh-so-sincere wisdom, proceeded to send the gospel of "greed for the few" though the ever-loving roof.

Is wanting a livable life for all hard-working Americans too much to ask for? Isn't that part of

America's promise? And does anyone *really* believe that anyone else running for president is going to grant it?

Dream! And Dream Big!

"The future belongs to those who believe in the beauty of their dreams."
Eleanor Roosevelt

Yes, we want Bernie Sanders in the White House, where his talents and spirit of service can do their most good. And, yes, we commit to doing whatever we can to help make that happen. So we begin with a *vision*: A "powerful beyond comprehension" *dream*. A lofty "shoot for the stars" image, bursting at the seams with idealism and all hocked up on possibility and promise. Visions, dreams, and other imagination-laced mental potions which are as potent as they are intoxicating.

To succeed at a goal as grand as ours is to first form a clear, emotionally-charged and sensory-rich vision of *what can be*. A picture that, through its clarity and certainty, literally draws us into tireless action and, at the same time, takes that churning yearning from our hearts and minds and, from it, fashions reality from its likeness.

So dream! Create that picture right now. Imagine our great and profound nation *finally* returning home to that which it was meant to be. A place where happiness – good, well-intentioned, benign happiness – can once again be pursued by all. Not just by the members of the 1%, or even the 2%, but by all of us.

Go ahead. Dream! Imagine President Bernie Sanders in Washington, fighting for all of us; working as he has for the past five decades for that which benefits the lives of working people throughout this great nation. Imagine him setting forth legislation that helps to bring us the better life we desire and work our butts off to attain; the better life which the mission statement of America purports to promise.

Go ahead. Dream! Get intoxicated by the thought that anyone with the desire, ambition, and effort can realize their potential by attending public college with neither the need for a privileged upbringing nor a future of crippling student loan debt. Imagine an America with so many more well-educated young adults. Imagine our country not only keeping up with the rest of the educated world, but, once again, leading it.

Dream of a government that, for once – for *once* – issues a resounding *no!* to corporate America's will to pollute with all the recklessness of a teenager tossing beer bottles out through the car window, to consume our resources, to destroy our ecosystem, to poison our air, water, and land, and to shift our climate ever closer to that of Venus.

Dream of a nation that pays all its workers a living wage. See them living lives with just a little less struggle and a little more ease. See that increased income circulating its way back into the economy and so creating even more prosperity for all, as it has done already in localities where higher minimum wages are in place.

Dream of a nation that values the health and well-being of all its citizens enough to take the bold step toward free universal healthcare (such as that which citizens in most other developed nations enjoy). Imagine what it means to live in a nation where families aren't left broken and bankrupt by grossly inflated healthcare premiums or out-of-pocket cancer treatment programs costing a million dollars or more. Imagine everyone being given the opportunity to get preventative and cost-saving health screenings. Imagine people beginning to take their prescriptions simply because they can now afford to.

Dream of a nation where we – the three-hundred-nineteen million men, women, and children who comprise it – come first once again. A nation that begins to put people before profits, people before greed, people before power.

So, before you begin doing what you can do to help put Bernie Sanders in the White House, look good and hard at your vision. Look at it again and again. Think about it day and night. Give it strength and energy and let it motivate and empower you to rise up to meet and master the rigors of the job that lies before you.

It is time to get motivated. It is time to energize our every action toward our shared goal of a Bernie Sanders presidency with the rocket fuel of our vision. This … is where victory begins.

Now let us take that rocket fuel and boost its octane even higher.

Get Mad

"In times of great stress or adversity, it's always best to keep busy, to plow your anger and your energy into something positive."
Lee Iacocca

Americans certainly have more than enough right to be angry. We have more than enough reason to be damn stinkin' mad. We pick up a newspaper, turn on the TV, or listen in on a heated roundtable discussion at the local doughnut shop ... and there it is: an ever-growing, ever-intensifying list of government and corporate infractions that incite our anger to ever greater degrees and continue to ratchet up our feelings of powerlessness.

"The rich get richer and the poor get poorer!"

Or, in its 21st century form: "The rich get over-the-top, out-of-control, *obscenely rich* and *everyone else* gets poorer!"

Of course they do. As the axiom states: Power corrupts. Greed can be the most addicting drug known to man. It has been that way throughout human history. But our industrialized modern times have brought with them a new, ever spiraling out-of-control degree of greed that is simply stupefying. It is a degree of greed that propels the members of the 1% into their lofty station by literally siphoning their wealth from working Americans whose stagnating wages fall ever further below cost-of-living increases, leaving millions in poverty.

In America?

Banks committing crime after unanswered-for crime. Wars waged for profit. Big pharma and big healthcare CEOs pulling in upwards of a quarter mil a day in salaries (while simultaneously breaking the backs of every premium-paying member). And all the while things get just a little worse for everyone else. A little worse here, a little worse there. A little more national debt to finance the wars and the Wall Street bailouts. A little less food on the table tonight because minimum and average wages don't even come close to keeping up with cost of living increases. A little more corruption this year. A bit hotter the global temps grow. A little more graft. A few more bridges falling down. A few more murmurings by the GOP that Social Security – *your* Social Security, which you pay into every week and which consists of money that is literally yours – just might be snatched from between your work-weary fingertips in order to finance yet another round of corporate bailouts and tax breaks for the wealthy.

And it's often almost too slow to notice or to perceive in real-time.

Almost.

Indeed, Americans *certainly* have things to be angry about.

Hopefully, in the years to come, beginning with a Bernie Sanders presidency, things will slowly start to move in the other direction.

But for right now, that anger that roils inside us has a positive facet. Anger, like all emotions, is a form of *energy*. Anger is the energy for change. So let us use it. Let's capitalize on it. Let's channel that anger into the energy for real and positive change. During the coming months before the election, let us harness that energy into potent, effective action to help Bernie Sanders get onto the ballot and into the White House.

Go ahead: Get mad.

Then … get busy.

Get Scared

"Don't be afraid of your fears. They're not there to scare you. They're there to let you know that something is worth it."
C. JoyBell C.

One of the reasons that there are so many climate-change deniers out there (aside from those who do it because it is in their financial best interest to deny through their teeth) is because the very concept of global climate change is *so* big and *so* frightening that, for many, it is virtually unthinkable. To many, it is best to simply deny it and hope it will go away.

It won't. It's like turning up the car radio to drown out the horrible noise coming from the engine in hopes that it will just go away.

Yes, climate change *is* scary. So, too, is the possibility of our teenagers being sent off to fight in yet another profit-motivated war. So is the threat of losing our Social Security. Americans have every right and every reason to be very afraid of these looming possibilities. But you don't ignore them. You elect leaders who are committed to *doing* something about them. Of course, in the case of global warming, you do what *you* can do as well in order to lessen your carbon footprint. Any steps you take, big or small, matter because they are mingled in along with like-minded steps taken by millions of other concerned and scared individuals.

But in matters of foreign policy, war-waging, Social Security legislation, or a minimum wage increase, it mostly comes down to *voting*: to electing those leaders with the experience, the capability, and the ethical standards with which to act upon these and other threats to our well-being.

So be afraid. Be very afraid. But don't pull the blankets over your head and hope that everything will just go away. Just shake it off, get out of bed, and get to work.

Get Smart

"Knowledge is power."
Francis Bacon

One thing that you will certainly discover as you talk to people about the upcoming election or the issues surrounding it: Altogether too many people think they're geniuses. You raise the issue of, say, corporations paying millions into candidates' campaign funds and they will fire right back with some cooked-up factoid they heard on Fox News as "proof" that you are wrong and they are intellectually superior. They will fight you tooth and nail into the wee hours because, again, they are right and you, the uninformed, non-Fox-viewer, are not.

Yes, some people actually regard Fox News malarkey as fact, no matter how often it is proven to be anything but.

Admittedly, talking to some people is like talking to a tree stump. No matter how smart you are on the issues, they're just plain smarter. That is perfectly fine; just write these people off. You simply cannot convince everyone that Bernie Sanders is not only the *best* choice we have, he is very much the *only* choice (that is, if you want to have a better life and all). But many, many people can, in fact, be swayed, just so long as you have your facts straight and not allow yourself to be out-talked.

So know your stuff. Know your talking points. And to make that happen: Read, read, and read some more.

First, if you haven't already done so, visit the Bernie Sanders website: www.berniesanders.com. Learn all about Bernie Sanders on the issues. Know what he's all about: facts, figures, and all.

Second, get your news from news organizations that *don't* conjure up their stories and points of view via the dictates of their corporate sponsors and/or who, themselves, are part of the 1% and who will filter any and all stories through the lens of corporate self-interest. Check out the following sites, along with any other progressive news organizations you might happen upon:

- Mother Jones: www.motherjones.com

- Alternet: www.alternet.org

- The Huffington Post:
  www.huffingtonpost.com

- Common Dreams:
  www.commondreams.org

- BuzzFlash: www.truth-out.org/buzzflash

- Air America Radio:
  www.airamericaradio.com

Finally, get a copy of each of these outstanding books, available everywhere:

Outsider in the White House (Bernie Sanders, John Nichols)

The Essential Bernie Sanders and His Vision for America (Johnathan Tasini)

Get informed. Get smart. Get savvy. Know you're stuff. Then, when an opportunity arises for you to express your opinions about Bernie Sanders and the 2016 election, you will be prepared to do so with solid, factual, comprehensive, and irrefutable viewpoint-altering information.

Get Big

> *"You have to think anyway, so why not think big?"*
> Donald Trump

Listen to the man! Listen to Donald. Just this once. Do it; think big. The man knows of that which he speaks (at least in matters of thinking big, which he is very good at). So do what he says ... again, just this once. Think big and dream big by imagining that a man as undeniably good to the core as Bernie Sanders will soon be President of these United States. Let us all think big by having the audacity to know, beyond the shadow of a doubt, that a winning presidential candidate doesn't need a bastion of billionaires backing him up, just millions of passionate, committed, and well-informed voters. And let us think big by presuming beyond the shadow of a doubt that our candidate can and will trounce Donald Trump, Hillary Clinton, or anyone else who gets in the way of We the People.

Another part of this whole "getting big" concept is the idea of getting *bold*, by getting *super-confident*. From now on you are to act with certainty. You are to speak with conviction. You are to "know like you know like you know" that Bernie Sanders can win, that he will win, and that he will win big – as in *really big*. If Donald Trump can sway his audiences solely through his absolute convictions, so can we.

So move through the coming weeks and months of the Bernie Sanders campaign with absolute, resolute assuredness that Bernie Sanders is the right choice and that he has what it takes to win this election and lead our nation to far greater things.

Get Pumped

"Nothing great was ever achieved without enthusiasm."

Ralph Waldo Emerson

Once again, working effectively toward a cause as monumentally important as electing Bernie Sanders to the presidency takes energy. And the greatest source of personal energy is *enthusiasm*. Bernie needs supporters who are pumped full of enthusiasm. Bernie needs supporters who are passionate about the issues because the issues which he cares deeply for and will fight for are the same issues that we care deeply for.

So get fired up. Passion and enthusiasm is effort multiplied – especially when we develop, as the late, great motivational author Napoleon Hill called it: "a white heat of desire." If you are already at that level, that's fabulous. May your enthusiasm be ever infectious and inspiring!

These are exciting times! The promise of universal healthcare, tuition-free public universities, a president willing to take on climate change, and a president who is beholden to no corporate agenda, having received no hefty donations from them in the first place ... it is all so compelling! So get enthusiastic, get fired up, and get passionate. Be a powerful part of the kind of voting electorate that the Bernie Sanders campaign can sure use.

Get Out There

"If you're not actively involved in getting what you want, you don't really want it."
Peter McWilliams

Powered with this high-octane rocket-fuel boost of energy – the kind which impassioned dreams, anger, fear, and strength can create – let us now get out there and do what it takes to make America great for the 99% again.

And don't think for a second that your actions will ultimately count for little. Bernie Sanders doesn't just have many millions of supporters on his side. He has many millions of supporters absolutely *lit on fire* on his side. He has, without question, cornered the market on voter passion, determination, and conviction in this election year.

Donald Trump may talk a good talk to his believers and stir up still more of that infamously misdirected anger of theirs. But that's all he has. His supporters are simply not in the same league as Bernie's when it comes to passion and enthusiasm. And anger, while an historically powerful motivator, will only get a candidate so far, especially in this day and age, when the attention span of an "angry" supporter is compromised by the latest hit movie or by working two jobs (in order, ironically, to compensate for Wall Street's and corporate America's siphoning of wealth to the 1%). They *might* go out and vote for Trump, but that's it. They are not going to "get out there" with anywhere near the same amount of passion or dedication as your typical Bernie Sanders supporter, nor will they vote in the same numbers. It ain't gonna happen.

The same goes for all the other candidates. Can you imagine a Hillary Clinton campaign *without* her Super PACs and other corporate money? Can you imagine her campaign operating, as does Bernie Sanders', solely on money from average citizens – and doing so without all of her assured corporate media attention? Think about that. It's downright laughable.

Imagine any other candidate doing what Bernie Sanders has done, with nothing more in their hands than what Bernie has. Our candidate gets no corporate funding, he receives almost no media attention, and the man still draws tens of thousands to his rallies – thirty thousand people so fired up they will drive a hundred miles through a blizzard to see him and, later, to vote for him.

Donald Trump, on the other hand, has a walloping amount of corporate and personal campaign cash, he is adored by the media, and still the guy can barely scrounge up a couple hundred "supporters" to attend one of his media circuses.

Sure, other candidates might do well in telephone polls. But are their followers going to go out there and vote in anywhere near the same numbers as Bernie Sanders' legions of supporters?

To think so is, again, laughable.

Furthermore, many Republican voters are growing increasingly disgusted with the dismal array of GOP candidates – candidates who have moved so far to the right and into the land of racial bashing, religious zealotry, and certifiable lunacy that they smell less like Republicans and more like fascists. Unfortunately, since many will continue to vote Republican simply out of habit and/or party loyalty – *even when doing so goes against their own best interest* – they end up "supporting" one candidate over the other simply because he or she represents the lesser of the evils.

This is *not* the sort of "support" that stirs a citizen to actually bother going out to vote.

Not so in the Bernie Sanders camp. Bernie Sanders supporters are enthusiastic, they're committed, and they're practically chomping at the bit to get inside that voting booth.

Thus, every Sanders supporter counts and counts big.

Every action taken by a Bernie Sanders supporter counts big as well.

Bigger than anyone else's.

Never forget that.

Stan Munslow

CHAPTER TWO
Action Steps Times Millions

"Never be afraid to raise your voice for honesty and truth and compassion against injustice and lying and greed. If people all over the world ...would do this, it would change the earth."
William Faulkner

Now it is time to act. It is time to spread Bernie Sanders' message of hope and opportunity to everyone you can. In the pages that follow, you will find specific actions that you can take in order to accomplish this goal. Do all of them. Do any of them. If you prefer, pick just one and devote yourself one hundred percent to carrying it out. The important thing is not how many steps you take or which ones you choose to take. What matters most is that you do, in fact, take a step, then another, and another still. What matters is that you move, along with the many millions of us who support Bernie Sanders, toward our shared goal of helping to elect this great man to the presidency.

It's a lot like getting into shape. It doesn't matter all that much which exercise shoes you by, which gym you join, which videos you buy, or which step aerobics program you follow. What matters is simply that you *move* – that you move your body hard and that you move it every day.

The same goes for us. Just move. Do what you can. Do whatever you can. Do it hard. And all the while know full-well that you are *not* one of the many who whine and complain about the state of the union, and then do nothing whatsoever about it. What, exactly, is the point of living in a democracy if we refuse to take part in that privilege beyond, perhaps, voting once every couple of years? Know that *you* are making a difference.

And know that you are now a part of history.

Get On the Air

> *"Nothing strengthens authority so much as silence."*
> Leonardo da Vinci

Do you deny the continuing power of radio? Perhaps you've not heard of, or forgotten about, that night back in 1938 when Orson Welles got on the air and, in doing a radio dramatization of H.G. Wells' "War of the Worlds," not only created panic among countless thousands of listeners (who believed that we were being invaded by Martians), but ultimately became a part of history for having done just that. Or, in a more modern context, ask yourself what would have become of every successful pop, rock, or country band without the power of radio?

Yes, television and the Internet now dwarf broadcast radio in magnitude. But, as the only information and entertainment medium available to those who are working, driving, or otherwise unable to look at a screen, radio is still alive and well and quite capable of greatly influencing public opinion.

This, of course, partly explains the continued popularity of radio talk shows. And this is precisely why you need to get on them as often as you can. Do not – again: *do not* – let those bastions of angry, mean-spirited conservatives – hosts and callers alike – make up the only "voice" heard on the radio. Get your facts, figures, and talking points assembled, rehearsed, and ready. Then start calling in any radio call-in show you can, conservative or not, and start talking. Stay calm, assertive, and confident. If the radio personality starts badgering you, don't get hostile. Let them rant and rave while you stick, gently but firmly, to your facts.

One of the best things you can say to any right-wing radio talk-show personality is something like this:

"I'm voting for Bernie Sanders because he is the only major candidate – *the only one* – who has *not* been bought out by the billionaires and the corporations. He is the *only* candidate without a Super PAC. He is thus the *only* candidate who is not beholden to Wall Street or the pharmaceutical companies or any other source of corporate-funded campaign money. Therefore, he is the *only* candidate who will do what's best for the

American people because his campaign is the *only* one financed *by* the American people."

If you get the chance, go on to mention universal healthcare. Mention free and debt free public college. Mention the idea of a minimum wage that can lift individuals out of poverty *and* stimulate the economy at the same time. Explain that these programs are very successful in many other developed countries, so why shouldn't Americans have the opportunity enjoy them as well?

These are very difficult statements to scoff at and equally difficult to refute. Nonetheless, conservative hosts will almost certainly scoff you and refute your statements (to put it mildly). This is to be expected. Respond if you wish, but don't allow yourself to get caught up in an argument. Just state your case and know that, no matter what the response from the host, the listeners will have heard your words, and will, quite possibly, be swayed by them.

Finally, get everyone you know to call in to these programs. Get friends and family members to call in to as many as they can and help put the name Bernie Sanders into the ears of every listener these programs have.

Write On

"Either write something worth reading or do something worth writing."
Benjamin Franklin

Letters to the editor of your local or regional newspaper are another great way to spread the word about Bernie Sanders. Just be sure to avoid any verbiage that resembles whining, desperation, belligerence, or self-righteousness, any of which are fairly certain to turn off readers, not to mention editors. Your best bet, as with call-in radio, is to simply state *why* you are voting for Bernie and to do so with enthusiasm, pure infectious enthusiasm. Enthusiasm sells; ranting or preaching … not so much.

If writing is not your thing, don't worry. Newspapers have editors who will fix sloppy grammar and the like. Besides, there is no need to write an essay. Just a couple of paragraphs are fine. Short is good. Short is very good, actually, and it is ultimately more hard-hitting and memorable, than a fluffed-up, long-winded diatribe.

If you are still unwilling to write on your own, invite a couple of friends over, order a pizza, and bang out a bunch of letters together.

It could be as simple as this:

Dear Editor:

I am excited about voting for Bernie Sanders because he is the *only* candidate who has not been bought out by the billionaires. He is the *only* candidate without a Super PAC. He is the *only* candidate not in the pocket of big business. He is the *only* candidate who will do what is best for the American people because his campaign is the only one financed exclusively by the American people. The other candidates' campaigns are paid by billionaires, lobbyists, and large corporations, so they will work, first and foremost, for the billionaires, lobbyists, and corporations. Senator Sanders' campaign is paid by the American people and will work, first and foremost, *for* the American people! He is a candidate whom all Americans can get behind, regardless of how they may have voted in the past.

You could go on to describe some of the planks in Bernie's platform such as the promise of free universal healthcare, a livable minimum wage, free public college tuition, breaking up the big banks, and/or whatever else about Bernie Sanders that inspires you, be it his agenda or his impeccable honesty, consistency, and efficacy. Add the point that many of the programs he is dedicated to bringing to America are already enjoyed by people in other countries, so why can't they be enjoyed by us?

Keep your sentences short and punchy. Keep your tone enthusiastic. And keep your writing simple. Your reason for doing this is to convince, not to impress.

In the end, it is more important that you do, in fact, write something positive about Bernie

Sanders, than how you word it, or which specific points you make.

Never forget that the pen truly is mightier than the sword.

Call or Email Television News Stations

"You can only watch injustice go on for so long until you're compelled to say something. To speak out against it."
Macklemore

As we know all too well, the broadcasting industry has decided in unison that a Bernie Sanders administration represents a supposed threat to their (and their sponsors') bottom lines. God forbid that corporation should actually have to do the unthinkable and actually pay taxes for a change. God forbid that their advertising friends in Detroit might have to start focusing their attention on more environmentally-friendly cars instead of their higher-markup, Hummer-esque SUVs. God forbid that Big Pharma corporations might have to rein in their hideous and absurd level of greed for once. And what is a defense industry player to do with a president who is actually unwilling to send his country's young people off to war (except, of course, as a last resort or in times to real crisis) so that they can sell a few dozen more of those really awesome billion-dollar fighter jets?

On one hand, it is perfectly understandable that the corporate news industry would choose to block covering the campaign of a man who is more pro-human than pro-corporate-excess. They are not in the news business to inform their viewers; they are there to make money.

The problem for them is that, in doing so, they are becoming the worst versions of themselves. They are beginning to look awfully bad to a whole lot of people. They are doing their jobs ever more poorly, with less and less a degree of professionalism. They, executives and commentators alike, are behaving more and more like greedy imbeciles, and, in this age of the Internet, they are making themselves appear increasingly irrelevant and unnecessary as a source of real news.

Alas, these points are of no concern, little concern, or perhaps simply less concern to them than the happiness of their and their advertiser's shareholders. And so the Bernie Sanders blackout remains in effect – and it will likely remain in effect until Bernie Sanders is seated comfortable at his desk in the Oval Office.

On the other hand, if enough viewers like you get angry enough and start calling or emailing the news networks, as well as their local affiliates, then their decision-makers just might start to listen.

Get started with any and all of the following (courtesy of www.nytix.com):

- Fox News: 212-301-3000.
  Email: comments@foxnews.com

- CNN: 1 (404) 827-1500.
  www.cnn.com/feedback

- CBS News: 202-457-4385.
  Email: evening@cbsnews.com

- ABC News: 202-456-7777.
  Email: netaudr@abc.com

- NBC News: 202-885-4259.
  Email: nightly@nbc.com

- MSNBC: 212-664-4444.
  Email: world@msnbc.com

What do you tell them? First, that their tactic of minimizing a leading candidate is blatantly self-serving and unprofessional. Second, that their blatant pandering to candidates who spew extremist, and often dangerous tirades is morally objectionable. Third, that you are now receiving your news online from more reliable and trustworthy sources.

This tactic, of course, offers no promise of success. But then, there is no guarantee that it *won't* work. In fact, if you simply refuse to watch their programs, opting instead to get your news from the BBC or the various online news outlets, then that would certainly begin to show up on their ratings and perhaps cause a few network execs (and their sponsors) to start shaking in their boots.

Ultimately, however, the very best response to the corporate media Bernie Sanders blackout is social media.

Social Media

"The Internet is becoming the town square for the global village of tomorrow."
Bill Gates

The Internet, along with its social media facet, is the big gun in Bernie Sanders' campaign arsenal. It is a primary source of information about Bernie, his beliefs and philosophies, his plans for America, his progress along the campaign trail, videos of his speeches and rallies, and more. Perhaps you were initially swept up and into the Bernie Sanders movement thanks to the Internet and social media.

So, please, do whatever you can to utilize these great resources to their fullest potential.

Facebook

For starters, take Facebook all the way. Post and repost Bernie Sanders videos and pro-Bernie postings. Share, share, and share some more. There are a mind-bogglingly huge number of powerful, well-designed, attention-grabbing and thought-provoking postings out there that deserve your help in spreading their messages. Like and/or join the following pages and you will receive a steady influx of informative and thought-provoking photos, articles, and soundbites for your liking, sharing, and reposting pleasure:

- Winning Democrats:
  www.Facebook.com/WinningDemocrats

- Bernie Sanders for President:
  www.Facebook.com/groups/BernieSandersAdmirers

- U.S. Senator Bernie Sanders:
  www.Facebook.com/senatorsanders

- Liberal and Proud of It:
  www.Facebook.com/LiberalAndProudOfIt

- Being Liberal:
  www.Facebook.com/beingliberal.org

- Occupy Democrats:
  www.Facebook.com/OccupyDemocrats

- Democracy Now:
  www.Facebook.com/democracynow

Read their content. Get informed. Get smart. Get even more riled up. Pick up a plethora of powerful new talking points.

Then, like them, comment on them, and share them on your page. Spread these messages far and wide and let the power and the magic of Facebook do its thing.

Then if you choose, design and write your own posts. Use graphics. Make your posts compelling. Make each one share-worthy, even potentially viral. Send your enthusiasm out into cyberspace. You never know who might be influenced by your messages.

Remember, the corporate media is, for the most part, doing nothing to inform the population of what Bernie Sanders is doing and what he is all about. On the contrary, they seem to delight in marginalizing this top contender. The Internet and social media comprise much of the antidote to their absurd posture. Many people know very little about Bernie Sanders. Indeed, some don't even know who he is or that he is, in fact, running for president. They just might like the idea of a candidate who really is in their best interest, rather than whichever "lesser of evils" they may currently be settling for, if, indeed, any. In addition, there are many who are being systematically and grossly misinformed by Fox News and other rightwing organizations about what Bernie Sanders is really about. They, too, could certainly stand to know the truth about what is going on in this important presidential race.

Because, as we know very well, to know the truth about Bernie Sanders is to come to realize that he really is the one that we, the 99%, really want in the White House. At the risk of redundancy, he is the only one who has not been bought and paid for by the billionaires; the only one who really will work for the American people.

Speaking of Facebook, don't forget that there are also many rightwing pages that you can visit. Why? First, it's always good to know what the other side is up to and how they think ("Know Thy Enemy."). Second, it never hurts to comment (in opposition, of course) on the many false, misleading, and destructive posts you will find there.

Try to do the bulk of your Facebook work during prime activity hours. According to Kissmetrics.com, Saturdays and noontimes appear to be the best choices. But, in the end, lots of activity on your part is certainly better than less.

Finally, don't forget to mention this book in your posts. Post quotes, excerpts, soundbites, anything that you feel will light up yet another regiment of Bernie supporters.

Twitter

Then there is Twitter. Too many pro-Bernie Tweeters to mention here, but seek them out, re-tweet any good stuff you find like crazy, and share the best tweets you find on Facebook (and vice-versa).

And, of course, tweet your own stuff as well. Join in on the trends and help to better spread your tweets by adding any of the following hashtags to any of your messages:

- #FeelTheBern

- #BernieSanders

- #Bernie2016

- #Bernie

- #Sanders2016

New to Twitter? Head over to: Twitter.com and follow the simple steps to set up your profile. Then, start spreading the news about America's next great president.

Here are some simple tweets to get you started:

- Free public college. Free universal medical care. $15 federal minimum wage. Bernie Sanders is the ONLY choice we have! Vote Bernie 2016!

- Surging in the polls. Tens of thousands at his rallies. Find out why at www.BernieSanders.com

- Are you sick of kooky GOP candidates and Hillary's close ties to her bank buddies? Come over to the Bernie Sanders revolution.

- Tired of bought and paid for presidential candidates? Bernie Sanders is the only one who isn't.

- Bernie Sanders for President 2016, or it's all for the billionaires again.

- Either Bernie Sanders wins or the billionaires win again. Can we afford to let that happen again?

- A buffoon, a bank buddy, or a Bernie Sanders revolution. The choice is ours! Learn more at: BernieSanders.com

- Admit it: You like socialism. You like Social Security, Medicare, fire departments, and public education. Bernie Sanders hears you!

- Name one candidate not owned by big money. Bernie Sanders. Name another. Time's up!

- Had enough? Bernie is the ONLY candidate not bought and paid for by big business. The only one who will work for YOU!

- Honest. Consistent. Experienced. Effective. It's Bernie Sanders … or nothing.

- Bernie is the ONLY candidate with an unshakable habit of telling the truth.

- Bernie Sanders is in it to win it. He is in it for all working Americans. Join the revolution at BernieSanders.com

- You see the mess George W. Bush made. And now you want another Republican? Seriously?

- Trump is real mean. Carson is real crazy. Clinton is real cozy with Wall St. Bernie Sanders is real.

- If you vote GOP/Hillary, then you must really like war, corporate greed, racism, low wages, and budget deficits. Bernie2016.

- Bernie Sanders is not for sale. Doesn't that feel good? www.BernieSanders.com

- Do you want Bernie Sanders – or more of the same? www.BernieSanders.com

- It's Bernie Sanders, or more of that "trickle up" economy that the GOP and Hillary love so much.

- Americans have HAD IT with corporations who pay no taxes. Come on over to the Bernie Sanders revolution.

- Do you seriously think there is one GOP candidate fit to lead this country? Seriously?

- You say you hate war. You hate unemployment. You hate budget deficits. You hate corporate greed. But you vote GOP. I'm confused.

- Quit being jealous of people in Denmark, with their free college & free healthcare. Vote for Bernie Sanders already!

- Bernie Sanders: "No one who works 40 hours a week should be living in poverty." www.BernieSanders.com

- Given his experience, integrity, wisdom, and commitment to the American people, Bernie Sanders could well become our greatest president.

- Spread the word! Only 1 candidate is not bought out by Wall Street. Bernie Sanders 2016.

- Feelin' the Bern? Get pumped! Get involved! Read "Many Millions Strong" by Stan Munslow.

Modify, edit, and personalize any of these. Then tweet and retweet away. Add those hashtags. Write your own, get creative, and have fun.

Become a lean, mean, tweeting machine!

Any of the above tweets would make great Facebook posts as well. The sky really is the limit with this. And when you multiply your efforts by the thousands – it is beyond mind-boggling.

Instagram, Etc.

Ditto for Instagram, MySpace, Google+, Tumblr, and/or any other social media platform you use. Post and repost, hashtag to the hilt, and create a Bernie Sanders cyber-awareness that takes the concept of viral to the moon and back.

If any friends or followers complain about your barrage of political posts, here are three things you can do:

1. Calmly explain that this is very important to you and that you need to do it for the sake of your future (and for the sake of your children).

2. Calmly explain that this is not about politics; it's about people, it's about jobs, it's about education, it's about the environment, and ultimately all of these things are about *us*.

3. Do your best to make your posts interesting, exciting, positive, and even fun in order to make it less likely that anyone will complain at all. Sure they may just skim over your content, but there is always that chance that something will catch their eye and they just might stop and read.

The bottom line is that the Internet and social media already are working wonders for the Bernie Sanders campaign and, with our help, they can do so much more. As everyone knows, one post can capture the world. Well, just think what millions of Bernie Sanders supporters, posting 24/7 for months on end can do.

This isn't "viral." This is nuclear.

Rally On!

"Where there is unity there is always victory."
Publilius Syrus

This is democracy in action, people! The more excited supporters attending rallies and events for Bernie Sanders, the more likely it is that newspapers and local TV stations will cover them. For any readers or viewers who still think that Bernie Sanders isn't a major player in this election, seeing thousands of supporters at his rallies (while at the same time seeing a paltry and pathetic few dozen or so at those of his rivals) can only help to give them second thoughts about our guy.

Needless to say, do not go alone. Organize a "Bernie Sanders Rally Group" at your place of employment, your college, or your church. At the very least, invite family members, friends, and neighbors. Go the extra mile by setting up a sign-making party beforehand.

Yes, there is work involved in this step, but just ask yourself: How important is this to me? Then do what needs to be done. Like the Olympic athlete with victory on the brain, you do whatever it takes.

And talk it up! Make attending the rally an event. Make it exciting for everyone. Enthusiasm is contagious. Say something like this to anyone who will listen: "You know, this is the first time in my life I've ever wanted to do something like this. Bernie Sanders is lighting up audiences wherever he goes and I really want to be a part of that incredible energy. Besides, it's history."

Finally, when you're there, don't let your excitement, energy, or enthusiasm wane for a second. Not that you will be able to; Bernie Sanders rallies and appearances typically get pretty darned exciting. Just let yourself get caught up in the energy and then stir in some of your own.

Find an event in your area here: https://go.berniesanders.com/page/event/searc h_simple

If there are no rallies scheduled within driving distance, do the next best thing by setting up a "pizza party online viewing night" with anyone you can get. And don't forget to have everyone tweet, post, and hashtag like crazy the whole time.

Excitement spreads like nothing else. Do your part to model that excitement, promote it, and fan the flames.

Flyers Still Work

*"What gunpowder did for war the printing press
has done for the mind."*
Wendell Phillips

Yes, indeed. Even in this age of digital everything, good old-fashioned flyers (and other printables) still work. Make your own or, better yet, visit www.FeelTheBern.org to access their flyer kit.

Download and print out all that you can. Post them wherever you have permission to do so. Get that "name recognition" thing going in the minds of those still sequestered away inside the Bernie Sanders corporate media blackout bubble.

But don't stop there. Download Bernie Sanders brochures at: www.berniesandersvideo. com/bernie-sanders-brochures.html.

Leave them everywhere you have permission to do so.

Buy a bumper sticker at The BernieSanders. com store: https://store.berniesanders.com/products.

This is also a great source for Bernie t-shirts and lawn signs.

Again, the important thing to remember is that if we don't go to this trouble to support our candidate in any and every way we can, rest assured that those on Bernie's well-funded opponent's side will. We absolutely cannot let them have the upper hand; this is far too important. There is so much at stake here that a few bucks spent on some paper, ink, and signage truly is an investment, not an expense.

So become a printing and plastering maniac. Print away as if your future depended on it (which, of course, it does). Plaster *Feel the* Bern messages far and wide. If *ever* there was a good cause … this is it.

Again, however, don't waste your time and money leaving flyers or brochures in places where they are neither welcome nor allowed. They will just get taken down, people will get angry, and you will get nowhere – or, worse yet, in trouble. Remember: when acting on behalf of a campaign built on such a high set of moral principles, it is all about acting with the sort of spirit and energy that complements this particular campaign. In every other candidate's campaign, it's all about stirring up feelings of fear, paranoia, hatred, divisiveness, greed, and other toxic energies. When building support for a man like Bernie Sanders, we are operating on a different wavelength; a higher plane. So it is vital that we infuse *our* actions with:

- Passion
- Positivity
- Enthusiasm
- Fervor
- Dedication
- Certainty
- Conviction
- Spirit
- Commitment

Do all that you do with these qualities and energies and they will infuse the Bernie Sanders election with more of the same.

That's powerful stuff.

If an action taken on your part and on Bernie Sanders' behalf does not reflect one or more of the above, it probably won't help and will, in any case, bring the wrong energy to this very important cause. Worse, if an action taken in this quest is taken with any degree of mean-spiritedness, or "stick it to the other guy" zealotry, or anything of the sort, it will invoke a negative force that neither Bernie nor we, his supporters, need.

In other words:

Act *out* of frustration, perhaps, but not *with* frustration.

Act with *spirit*, but not *mean-spiritedness*.

Let your anger *energize* your actions, but don't let it *define* them.

Leave all the negative energy and mean-spiritedness to the GOP supporters. When acting on behalf of Bernie Sanders, act in the spirit of Bernie Sanders by rising to his level of decency and positivity.

Organize a Mall Walk

"Many a small thing has been made large by the right kind of advertising."
Mark Twain

Here is a terrific idea that's begun to spring up around the country: First, gather a group of friends, coworkers, family, and neighbors. Then go to www.berniesanders.com and order t-shirts and signs for everyone.

Then … hit the malls

Sporting Bernie Sanders t-shirts and mile-wide smiles, arrive at a prime time for mall traffic. If your group is larger than, say, eight or nine people split up into groups and hit those concourses without appearing overpowering or disconcerting to anyone. Obviously, don't solicit or badger people in any way, shape or form either. Your mission is simply to get Bernie's name – and your enthusiastic and contagious support for him – seen by a lot of people. Of course, if anyone approaches *you* with questions or comments, then by all means engage with him or her. Carry flyers or brochures and hand them out to anyone who asks.

What a fun, spirited way to spread the word! And that is the key: Fun. Have fun, be spirited, be friendly, be positive, be energized, be approachable. Infuse your presence with the same spirit as that of the Bernie Sanders campaign at large.

And malls are just the beginning. Any place where people congregate – any appropriate venue – is great. Outdoor shopping areas, busy train stations, festivals, piazzas, tourist areas, pedestrian concourses, and so on. Take a look around your area and see what looks good.

Every hour you spend at this particular task will do wonders for the campaign, burn off some calories, and be a source of pure pleasure you'll never forget.

Give Generously

"Real generosity toward the future lies in giving all to the present."
Albert Camus

Bernie Sanders' campaign is financed exclusively by his supporters: *We the People* who believe in Bernie. *We the People* who know, deep in our hearts, that the greatest country on Earth should do all it can to provide for everyone the opportunity to enjoy the greatest quality of life on Earth. A life with more opportunity, more hope for peace, and more income in our pockets with which to circulate back into our economy. A life with less stress and hardship over medical premiums and costs, less damage to our irreplaceable, life-sustaining ecosystem, and less erosion to our infrastructure.

So now you must ask yourself: How much is a Bernie Sanders presidential victory worth to me?

To my family? The price of two lattes? A nice dinner? A month of cable? You decide. But no matter what you decide, no matter how much you can give, or how little, know that it will be *greatly appreciated* by Bernie and his election committee and it will, most certainly, make a difference – unlike with other presidential candidates who will gladly take it, but who will save their excitement for the big corporate "contributions." With Bernie Sanders, We the People are *the* source of campaign money. Therefore, *we* matter; our contributions matter.

And, as we are many millions strong, our contributions, combined together, matter even more.

And that is how it will always be with Bernie Sanders in the White House. It's about us. It's about "we." What he does as president will be done for us; it will matter greatly to us. And what *we* do to help him do his job will always matter and matter greatly. Remember: America will no longer be about the corporations. America will no longer be about the oligarchy. It will be about the three hundred nineteen million human beings who make up this great nation. Whether we're doing the giving: by helping Bernie do his job, or the receiving; by enjoying the "New and Improved" United States of America that he will work toward building (just as he's always done throughout his many years of public service), one way or another, it will always come down to: We the People.

And it all starts right now by investing in our future with any donation you can make to the Bernie Sanders campaign. Whether it is a one-time donation, or a recurring donation, please support this great man. Log on to www.BernieSanders.com and give what you can. It is a safe bet that you will feel very good about doing it.

Volunteer!

Want to get some serious involvement going? Would you like to volunteer for the Bernie Sanders campaign for real? Visit: https://go.berniesanders.com
Here you will have the opportunity to officially participate in any of following:

- Leafleting voters

- Knocking on doors

- Working in a campaign office

- Tabling events

- Hosting a meeting or fundraiser

- Hosting or attending a house party

- Helping out in many other ways that suit your talents, interests, and schedule

No matter which activity or activities you choose, you are sure to get an incredible feeling of satisfaction both from having contributed to such an exciting and historic cause as well as the opportunity to share the experience with other dedicated and like-minded individuals. The experience is sure to be rewarding.

Go for it. Sign up today. Then roll up your sleeves and get started.

Many Millions Strong

"It's when we start working together that the real healing takes place ... it's when we start spilling our sweat, and not our blood."
David Hume

Never forget that every time you act on behalf of the Bernie Sanders campaign, your effort is multiplied times the many thousands of like actions being carried out by other Bernie Sanders supporters.

When you call in on a radio talk show, know that many other people are doing the same.

When you post on social media, you are adding your voice to the chorus of millions singing "We want Bernie!" – giving that chorus even more power, more dimension, and ultimately more effectiveness.

When you distribute "Feel the Bern!" flyers and brochures, you are joining with a veritable army of Bernie Sanders volunteers doing the very same thing.

No matter what the action, the rush you will get from carrying it out "alongside" your many thousands of coworkers, along with the feelings of contribution to an important cause, and participation in an historic undertaking, are sure to be nothing short of life-changing.

Any action, big or small, times many, is a very big action. It truly is the very sort of action from which revolutions are borne.

Stan Munslow

CHAPTER THREE

Work That Law of Attraction

"With our thoughts we make our world."
Buddha

Chances are, you're heard something about the phenomenon known as The Law of Attraction, particularly during the past several years since the movie *The Secret* brought it into public awareness, after remaining locked away in the world of the intelligentsia, the super-rich, and the super-success-minded for millennia. Here it is in a nutshell:

We attract to us that which we focus on.

With our thinking, we create our reality. But not just any old thinking. It is with our deep, persistent, continual, emotionally-charged thinking that we truly create our world. Now remember: this is not theory, it is not "new age." This is science: as real and as scientifically proven as the law of gravity. This is science which even the likes of Einstein and today's quantum physicists the world over have acknowledged and embraced. Thus, you would do well to embrace it as well and harness the power of this universal law for the good of this historic presidential race.

It has been said by more than one Law of Attraction pundit that Donald Trump himself utilizes the Law of Attraction in the creation of his immense wealth, be that consciously or unconsciously. How else can one explain how a man could lose billions, then, within the span of a few short years, get it all back again? If this is the case, there is every possibility that Mr. Trump is already calling upon this immense power in his own fight for the Oval Office.

Admittedly, he may be effective at utilizing the Law of Attraction, but we are many millions strong! If *we* were to invoke the Law of Attraction in our support for Bernie Sanders, miracles will happen.

Harnessing the Law of Attraction is about *focusing your thinking*. It is about keeping your thoughts firmly and unwaveringly fixed upon a Bernie Sanders landslide victory. Conjure up that vision of this victory that we discussed earlier and keep it lodged securely in your thoughts. Picture him seated at his desk in the Oval Office. Obsess on this vision. Pray on it.

Most important: Keep it *emotionally charged*. This cannot be stated strongly enough. It is not so much the thoughts of victory themselves that make the Law of Attraction happen. It is the energy which our deep, passionate emotions infuse into these thoughts that can and does move mountains.

So, every time you imagine that magical night of November 8, 2016, when it is announced that Bernie Sanders has just been elected, by a landslide, as the 45th President of the United States, or any other winning moment along his path to victory, pump that vision up with the same degree of joyful excitement you are sure to experience on that night to come. Infuse your Bernie Sanders victory daydreams and ruminations with all the powerfully intense emotional energy you can.

Think with:

- Excitement
- Exhilaration
- Elation
- Joy
- Jubilance
- Glee

Furthermore, fill your thoughts with *gratitude*. Feel deeply grateful over the upcoming Bernie Sanders landslide victory. Begin to feel grateful for that soon-to-be-realized victory even now. What we experience in our inner world, we ultimately experience in our outer, physical reality.

The Universe gives you more of that which you are grateful for.

This last sentence should be restated at least a hundred more times in this book. It is *that* important.

The Law of Attraction has been harnessed by countless individuals throughout history to amass great wealth, cure "incurable" diseases, and help ensure athletic victories. It works. It is real. It has worked for centuries, indeed, throughout human history. And quantum physicists have scientific-ally proven this to be true.

So when you conjure up visions of a Bernie Sanders victory know this: your thoughts are moving out into the Universe, merging with the thoughts of many, many people, and helping to create the physical equivalent of these thoughts: a Bernie Sanders landslide victory.

The Law of Attraction is *real*. Believe in it like you believe in the sun rising in the morning. Know it with every cell in your being.

Another important point: Never, ever entertain the notion of failure. To focus on failure is to attract failure. Dream with nothing but *absolute certainty* in victory for Bernie Sanders. Visualize with utter conviction. Do not "hope." Do not "wish." Simply *know* it as fact. Know that this reality will come to be. Do this by imagining over and over that it, in fact, already has.

Help ensure a Bernie Sanders victory by imagining over and over that it has already come to be.

And remember, if we don't harness this power for the good of the Bernie Sanders campaign, someone else will more than likely harness it for theirs.

Visualize Victory – Often and Hard

"Dare to visualize a world in which your most treasured dreams have become true."
Ralph Marston

As often as you possibly can, focus on visions of a Bernie Sanders presidential victory. Send those thought vibrations out into the Universe every chance you get. Lace that vision with clarity, sensory detail, intensity, and powerful emotion.

Remember, any action, no matter how small, times millions, is huge. It is powerful – unfathomably powerful.

Here are two visualization prompts to get you started:

It is primary season. On the night of each state battle, you sit in your favorite chair, your attention riveted upon the TV screen. You watch as the numbers pile up in the Sanders column, blowing all contenders out of the water. You whoop it up as the reporters and anchors announce yet another Sanders victory with shock and awe all over their faces. You see Bernie Sanders, along with his wife Jane, the two smiling broadly. You celebrate the victory with a knowing smile, as you knew all along in your heart that it would turn out just like this. Indeed, it was never even close. Bernie Sanders has just enjoyed yet another walloping victory. You celebrate this latest victory with deep gratitude, ever aware that the Universe gives us more of that which we are grateful for – especially when it is times millions.

Now, it is election night. You, your family, and your friends are gathered for a Bernie Sanders victory party. Everyone's eyes are glued to the TV, watching those electoral votes on the screen fall decidedly into the Bernie Sanders column. State after state falls to Bernie. Even traditionally red states come crashing down in in the Democrats' favor. It seems almost too easy. But there is the proof: those electoral votes heading rapidly toward that all-important 270 … then … BOOM! Right through that number and beyond they go! Again, you whoop it up and you smile with satisfaction at that by-now familiar look of shock and awe on the faces of the reporters – the reporters who had ignored Bernie Sanders all along and played up his opponent with blind allegiance. Now there they are using the term "President Elect Bernie Sanders."

Yes, *President Elect Bernie Sanders.* Doesn't that sound fabulous? Keep playing those words in your mind.

Now hear those reporters:

"President-elect Bernie Sanders has just received the call from *(insert name of crushingly-defeated GOP candidate here)* conceding defeat."

"President-elect Bernie Sanders has just arrived outside the ballroom and is expected to make his victory speech in just a few moments."

"The room is absolutely wild with excitement! President-elect Bernie Sanders is now standing at the podium, waving to the crowd and smiling as he waits and waits ... and waits ... for the cheering to subside."

History has been made. You toast this incredible moment with jubilation.

This is the Law of Attraction in action. *"With our thoughts, we make our world."*

And when those thoughts are the coalesced thoughts of many millions strong, there really is no doubt whatsoever that they will manifest in reality. When those thoughts are the powerful, focused, persistent, and impassioned thoughts of many millions strong ... a *New and Improved* America is just around the corner.

Stan Munslow

CHAPTER FOUR

For God's Sake, Vote!

"Elections belong to the people. It's their decision. If they decide to turn their back on the fire and burn their behinds, then they will just have to sit on their blisters."

Abraham Lincoln

It boggles the mind to consider how many millions of people say they "like" so-and-so for President … and then, come Election Day, don't even bother to vote – neither for that candidate nor anyone else. Of course, following the election, barely a day will go buy during which these same individuals won't be complaining nonstop about this president or that president or about the way things are being handled in this country. The rest of us can only stand there, shaking our heads, thinking: *seriously*?

Republicans tend to win during elections with low voter turnout. 2016 must NOT be one of those election years. Vote! For God's sake. For our sake. For the sake of our children. For the sake of the planet. If you do nothing else mentioned in this book, please vote for Bernie Sanders.

If anyone has *ever* deserved your vote, Bernie does. Other candidates have *wanted* your vote, to be sure. But Bernie Sanders is the only candidate in many a year who actually deserves it.

What does this mean? Bernie will take your vote and, after he becomes president, he will make your vote count by working for *you*. Who else is going to do that? Answer: no one. Every other candidate will take your vote, then turn around and act on the behalf of those who financed his campaign, not for those who voted for him or her. Certainly there will be a lot of talk about doing this and that for the American people. Perhaps even a few pieces of positive legislation will be signed, and possibly passed, to make it appear as though we, the 99%, are being well looked after. Then … it will be right back to business as usual; back to the business of making sure that the oligarchy is being very well looked after.

Because, as Americans know all too well, the billionaires, banks, and big businesses require a lot of care, special treatment, and unending accommodations.

But with Bernie Sanders at the helm, it will be a whole other story.

Never in many years has your vote counted quite this way. Never in many years has it counted for so much. A vote for Bernie Sanders is a vote for our future. A vote for anyone else is a vote for the financial elite. A vote for anyone else is a vote for someone who promises this or that, then, once in power, will act primarily on the behalf of those who pumped the most moolah into their campaign. And rest assured: their agenda will be a pro-business, pro-money agenda, no matter what else it may pretend to be.

Like the old saying goes: "Whenever a politician speaks, no matter what they're talking about, they're talking about money."

So yes, vote. Vote for the rare exception to that saying. Vote for Bernie Sanders with your heart and soul and know that we, the American People will ultimately benefit.

And don't stop there.

Please go the extra mile. Encourage friends, family, and co-workers who share your values to make sure that they actually vote for Bernie as well. Offer rides to seniors, the differently-abled, and anyone who might need a ride to the polling place.

Finally, don't forget to vote for a congress and senate who will work with Bernie Sanders. Let's give him a solidly Democrat house and senate to work with. Of course, there are likely to be many Bernie Sanders supporters who will then turn and vote for GOP representatives, rationalizing that they "vote for the person," that the two parties are the same anyway, so what difference does it make?

Nothing could be further from the truth.

Nothing could be more erroneous. Look at any congressional or senate vote by party and you will see, all too clearly, that Democrats resoundingly fall on the side of the working people. Not all the time, of course, but much of the time. Representatives typically vote along party lines; again, not always, but typically.

Bottom line: A Democrat-led House and Senate will go a long way toward helping Bernie Sanders do the job for which he was hired.

PART TWO

KNOW YOUR STUFF

"Silence becomes cowardice when occasion demands speaking out the whole truth and acting accordingly."

Mahatma Gandhi

Stan Munslow

CHAPTER FIVE

Talking Points and Responses

"People should not underestimate me."
Bernie Sanders

Following is an array of facts, figures, sound bites, and talking points to help you spread the word about Bernie Sanders with clarity, accuracy, and influence, as well as responses to anyone who may argue with you or otherwise be in error.

But first, here is a warning:

Often, when people come out in defense of Bernie Sanders, they do so with an air of self-righteousness that's just downright off-putting. Or, they'll become defensive, combative, and disrespectful of other people's opinions, erroneous or not.

No one enjoys being preached to. No one appreciates being corrected or told that they're wrong.

Furthermore, stay away from any behavior that might be perceived by an average person as "extremist."

Say, for example, that someone lashes out with: "Oh, that Bernie Sanders is a socialist!" Don't jump on a soapbox and start preaching ad-nauseam about how Socialism is the superior political system that will change the world. Whether this speculation is, or would ever be, true, your ranting will more than likely backfire. People have been misinformed about the "evils" of socialism for their entire lives. Often they hear the term "socialism" and, instead of thinking: *Norway*, they confuse the term with "communism" and wind up thinking: *Soviet Union*. The best you can do is to simply shrug and respond with something like: "Well, but, you know something? The U.S. is already a social democracy – in so many ways. We already have socialized education, a socialized postal service, Social Security, and Medicare. Oh, and FDRs New Deal basically saved the country. Not exactly a bad thing."

For an extra zinger you could always add: "Besides, you want to talk about a big socialist program, how about that bank bailout in 2008 that cost us seven hundred billion! Why should big business have socialist programs and not us – especially when a quarter of these corporations don't even pay one penny in income taxes?"

So do stay clear of any confrontational or self-righteous modes of delivery when spreading Bernie's message. At best, you will most likely annoy your listeners. At worst, it will incite them to dig in their heels and possibly vote for the other guy just out of spite towards you.

Yes, we're angry. And perhaps we have every "right" to vent our anger. But consider the following:

First: Having the "right" to be angry at certain abuses of government or corporate power, doesn't mean you have the "right" to direct this anger at others simply because you disagree with them. Chances are, they are simply the way they are because they watch Fox News or some other rightwing program and have been systematically misinformed, even brainwashed, for years on end. In any case, your anger will get you nowhere. Second, since lashing out is seldom productive (and sometimes dangerous), avoid it, whether it feels justified or not. It is almost certainly not going to help our cause.

To put it bluntly: Do you want to be right, or do you want to help get Bernie Sanders into the White House?

Once again, anger is a useful tool with which to energize ourselves in order to work hard on this campaign. But that is where we all must draw the line. Get energized. Then act. But don't pick fights. And even if someone tries to pick a fight with you or says something that angers you, be the better person by not sinking to their base level. State your views and if someone tells you that you're wrong, remain calm, cool, and level-headed. Then say something like: "Well, I guess we all get our news from different sources, don't we?"

Then, it may be best to just leave. There are many, many individuals who are simply so entrenched in their thinking that trying to change their mind is a complete waste of time. And we don't have a lot of time to waste.

The best posture you can have in any exchange of words, whether with an opponent or ally, is to:

1. Remain calm at all times. Seriously, a calm exterior carries more authority.

2. Be well-informed. Be very-well informed. Know your facts.

3. Model enthusiasm. Enthusiasm is very contagious.

4. Likewise, model passion and conviction.

5. Avoid anything the other person might consider "extremist" or "out there." This will only alienate them further.

6. Speak in terms that align with your listener's values. Speak about issues of concern with them. For example, if your listener drives a Hummer, chances are that speaking out about the environmental aspects of Bernie's agenda will fall upon deaf ears. But focusing on saving Social Security or breaking up the big banks just might get you in.

Sadly, not every person hearing your words will be swayed by them, no matter how adroitly you deliver them. Some will tune you out. Some will tell you to shut up. Some will tell you that you're an idiot. But you just keep putting the promise of a Bernie Sanders presidency out there and putting it out there and putting it out there.

Sometimes your words will stick. Sometimes they won't. But you just keep plugging. Then, at some point in the very near future, your words and the words of every other Bernie Sanders supporter will, together, reach a critical mass which, by the grace of God, will shake this country to the core, wake people up, and move that needle steadily and ever closer toward its target:

Bernie Sanders, 45th President of the United States of America.

Here Is What You Say

"No matter what people tell you, words and ideas can change the world."
Robin Williams

When speaking on the subject of:

Income and wealth inequality

You might say …

- You know, since the 1980s there has been **a huge transfer of wealth from the poor and middle class to the super rich.** The U.S. may be the "wealthiest" country on Earth, but since most of that wealth is concentrated in the hands of the top 1%, this means virtually nothing to almost anyone else.

- Bernie will *reduce* income inequality by **making the wealthy and large corporations pay their fair share in taxes**. That would be nice for a change, wouldn't it?

- Bernie will **stop corporations from moving jobs and profits overseas**, which many of them do all the time in order to avoid paying taxes.

- Bernie will also **tax Wall Street speculators** whose dirty deals cost us our jobs, our savings, and our homes.

- The U.S. minimum wage lags far behind inflation rates. **Bernie will increase the federal minimum wage from $7.25 to $15 an hour by 2020**. This isn't about "teenagers making more money," by the way; the bulk of minimum wage earners happen to be adults and single moms.

- **Raising the minimum wage to $15 an hour is better for the economy as well** because the more money people earn, the more goods and services they buy. Also, the more people earn, the more taxes they pay, and the less we spend on food-stamps and other programs to help the poor. It's a win-win.

- In the Unites States of America, **no one who works full-time should have to live in poverty**. That's morally wrong don't you think?

- Bernie will put millions of Americans to work by investing $1 trillion towards **rebuilding our crumbling infrastructure** – roads, bridges, airports, rail systems, and so on.

- Bernie will invest $5.5 billion in creating **one million jobs for disadvantaged young Americans.** It's a lot like FDR's WPA, the Works Progress Administration. Talk about helping the country!

- Women earn only about seventy-eight cents to each dollar earned by a man. Bernie will fight for **equal pay for women** with the Paycheck Fairness Act.

- Unions have a history of fighting for better jobs and higher wages for their members. They have done so much over the years to improve working conditions for all Americans. Bernie will work for the Employee Free Choice Act to **make it easier for workers to join unions**.

- Bernie will fight for legislation that will **break up the big banks** so that they are no longer too big to fail (to the tune of hundreds of billions of taxpayer dollars) as was the case in 2008.

- Don't ideas like this make a lot of sense? **How to pay for them?** Closing offshore tax havens that big businesses use to avoid paying their fair share of taxes will make a huge dent in those costs. Reducing our runaway military spending, which now accounts for more than half of our entire budget, will help a lot, too.

Improving our quality of life

- Bernie Sanders wants America to be more academically competitive by making **public colleges and universities tuition-free**. If someone has the ambition to learn, they shouldn't have to miss out on an education because of their inability to afford one. Shouldn't we have the best educated people on the planet?

- With many more people going to college, it is a safe bet that they will **obtain better-paying jobs** after college. The more money they earn, the more they will pay in taxes.

- If someone has completed college success-fully, does it sound fair that they should be rewarded by being strapped with **years of student debt** just when they're trying to begin their adult lives?

- Senior poverty rates are increasing. Bernie wants to **expand Social Security by lifting the cap on taxable income above $250,000.** He says that everyone should be able to retire with dignity and I happen to agree with that.

- No one should suffer bankruptcy or go into severe debt because they get sick. The U.S. is the only major industrialized country that doesn't guarantee healthcare as a right of citizenship. Bernie will enact a **Medicare for all single-payer healthcare system.**

- **People in other developed countries have free universal healthcare.** And although they pay for this healthcare through tax money, they ultimately pay a lot less because there are no HMOs scraping billions off the top for themselves.

- Bernie will require employers to provide at least **twelve weeks' paid family and medical leave, two weeks of paid vacation, and seven days' paid sick days.** Having the time to care for your children and ill family members is a privilege enjoyed by citizens in other developed countries. Why shouldn't we in the United States be allowed to enjoy the same privilege?

- Bernie will enact a **universal childcare and prekindergarten program**. This will help give our children the best start in life that they can possibly have. Anyone with young children would want that.

- Look, I have kids. The last thing I'm going to do is vote for someone who is pro-war, pro-gun, anti-environment, anti-affordable college, or anti-worker. **I want my children to have a safe and prosperous future.**

- Many other countries enjoy programs like these. **We live in the greatest nation on Earth. Shouldn't we have the opportunity to enjoy the greatest lifestyle on Earth?** Why should U.S. citizens have to live under the stress of massive healthcare premiums or decades of student debt?

On the environment

- **If you care about the state of the environment, Bernie is** *by far* **the best choice.** We all know where the GOP candidates stand: "Global warming? What global warming?" Bernie Sanders has a very impressive record in working for the health or our environment such as securing funding to reduce greenhouse gas emissions.

- **Bernie Sanders has one of the best environmental voting records in the Senate.** No other presidential contender even comes close.

- The "climate debate" really is over. An overwhelming majority of climate scientists agree that climate change is real. Bernie will **ban fossil fuel lobbyists from operating in the White House**, influencing elected officials, and building climate change skepticism.

- Bernie will **end taxpayer-funded subsidies to the fossil fuel industry**.

- To some degree or other, **every other presidential candidate is paid by the fossil fuel industry**. They will say or do anything in order to help their campaign backers. Bernie is the only candidate on the side of the American people – their health and well-being.

- Bernie Sanders understands that **global warming is a contributing factor to terrorism and international conflict**. That is why he plans to invest in clean, sustainable energy while at the same time moving our nation away from the planet's dwindling supply of fossil fuels.

If anyone tells you that "socialism is evil"

- First of all, Bernie is a *Social Democrat*. Countries like those in Scandinavia that have advanced social programs rank significantly higher than the U.S. in overall happiness.

- Forbes Magazine ranks Denmark, a social democracy, as the number-one best country for business. Other social democracies such as Sweden, Norway, and Finland also rank far above the U.S. in that regard.

- We already have many social programs such as public education, Social Security, Medicare, and socially-funded fire and police departments. But wouldn't it be great to have tuition-free college and free medical care, as they do in most other developed countries? Wouldn't losing those burdens greatly improve our quality of life?

- Wouldn't it be better for families to have paid maternity leave and paid childcare like other countries do? Why should others enjoy these advantages and not Americans?

- I hear Republican's talking about Bernie giving "free stuff" to everyone. Well, the GOP has made a career giving free stuff to the 1%. Besides, it's not "free stuff." Social programs that help people are paid by our tax money! It's not free. We pay taxes, we get to decide where that tax money goes, and I say it goes to us, not the 1%.

If someone accuses you of being anti-business

- No, actually I happen to be very much pro-business. What I am against is corporate excess and corporate abuse of power. What I'm against is the **large number of corporations who don't pay their taxes**, who take billions from our government, and us, in the form of handouts, who don't act in accordance with environmental regulation, and who try to steal elections in order to sway our leaders away from acting in the best interest of the population

- No, I am very pro-business. **I want people to earn enough so that they can buy the goods and services offered by corporate America.**

- Bernie Sanders proposes a $15 minimum wage, which will not only help individuals and families, but will greatly help the economy as well as American business by **giving more Americans more buying power.**

- A $15 minimum wage will help **circulate money back into American business** and help fuel our economy and employment. More income equals more consumer spending.

If someone says that people who live in countries like Denmark pay more in taxes for their enviable social programs

- Yes, they do. But they really don't mind. Think about it: Americans hate paying taxes because they seldom receive any benefit from them. Most of the money goes to offset losses from offshore corporate tax havens, corporate subsidies, over-the-top defense spending, and so on. It's a whole different story when, in a country like Denmark, your tax money pays for *your* medical needs, *your* education, childcare, and other programs that benefit *you*. **Your tax money goes to *you*, not to big business.**

- Paying taxes isn't the problem. We will always pay taxes. It's a matter of whether we allow our tax dollars to be spent helping corporations to rake in even more money, or **investing our tax dollars in programs that benefit all of us**.

- **Where would you rather see your tax dollars go? To the banks and the billionaires? Or to you and your children?** It is as simple as that.

If someone says that Donald Trump or Ben Carson is "so great!"

- Well, I can't vote for these men because **neither Trump nor Carson has any experience in government whatsoever.** To me, that's like hiring a pastry chef to fix your furnace. It would be like hiring auto mechanics to educate our children. I want someone with experience – someone with a history of fighting for us. I want someone who will be respected internationally and who really understands how government works. I don't really feel that the U.S. presidency is the place for someone who has zero experience in Washington, zero experience in government, and zero experience in diplomacy.

- People talk about how great it would be to have an "outsider" in the Oval Office. But, seriously, they wouldn't have a clue how to operate in government or how to work with the legislature. Besides, **Bernie Sanders, even with his decades of experience in government, is the best kind of outsider.** He operates outside the "money machine" that causes others in government to put the needs of citizens below the needs of the oligarchy.

- The presidency is no place for someone who has zero experience in law, politics, government, international relations, or leadership.

- I'm sorry, but **neither a surgeon nor a businessman has what it takes to be entrusted with leading the world's most powerful nation**.

If someone says that Hillary Clinton is the best choice for Democrats

- The problem with Hillary Clinton is that she is so similar to the Republicans, many people refer to her as one. Her receiving huge donations from the same interests and corporations that donate to GOP candidates means that, once in office, **she will work on *their* behalf more than ours, just as she's always done.** If you want real change in Washington – change that puts people before profit – Hillary is not the person for that job.

- **Yes, this country is certainly ready for a woman President, but not Hillary**.

- **So you believe that someone receiving millions and millions of dollars from Wall Street, the pharmaceutical companies, and weapons manufacturers is going to work in *your* best interest?** That she's going to put your needs ahead of those of her donors? Ain't gonna happen.

- **Hillary Clinton may have experience in government, but it's the wrong kind of experience**. She is quite experienced in working with the big banks and big business. She is very experienced in helping those *more* fortunate.

- Unlike Hillary, **Bernie is not for sale!**

If someone hits you with "I can't vote for Bernie because I'm a Republican"

- So you're going to continue to vote for candidates who want to take away *your* Social Security just because you've always voted Republican in the past? I can't do that. I can't vote against my own best interest just because of a candidate's label, Republican or Democrat. I vote for the man, not the party. And, to me, seeing the bulk of my tax money going to banks and other big businesses instead of programs that help people is a pretty big issue.

- You mean, you're going to vote against your own best interests, for someone you don't even like, because of a self-chosen label? Good luck with your Social Security, your medical insurance premiums, and your student loan debt.

- Then I have to ask: Have you gotten a good return on your party affiliation? Have Republicans *really* done a great job leading this country? Look at George Bush. Look at George W. Bush. Look at the voting records of House and Senate Republicans. You seriously want more of that?

- I refuse to vote for a candidate who calls himself or herself a Republican, but who operates so far on the extreme right, it's actually scary. It's time for a change, wouldn't you say?

- The GOP supports and gives subsidies to corporations who don't even pay taxes. That doesn't bother you?

Bernie really cares for our Veterans

- Frankly, I'm tired of hearing candidates talk endlessly about getting the U.S. into yet another war, then **turn on our veterans by slashing funding for programs that offer them assistance**. That is criminal in my view.

- **Bernie Sanders wants to expand the VA** so that every veteran gets the care that he or she has earned and deserves.

- **Bernie has introduced legislation to restore all cuts in military pensions.** He will also expand the VA's Caregivers program and expand mental health services for veterans.

If someone says "I saw it on Fox News"

- I would be very careful about that. According to PunditFact, Fox News makes half-true statements 19% of the time, mostly-false statements 21% of the time, false statements 29% of the time, and very false statements 9% of the time. **Fox News statements are true or mostly true only 22% of the time.**

- You know, given Fox News' proven track-record on spewing misinformation, I don't really think of them as a news network. To me, **Fox is more like "The Enquirer" of television.**

Zingers and one-liners

Note: These are essentially the same as those shown in the section on suggested Twitter tweets, but they make good conversation starters as well.

- Free public college. Free universal medical care. $15 federal minimum wage. The way I see it, Bernie Sanders is the only choice we have.

- Bernie is surging in the polls. He draws tens of thousands at his rallies. Find out why at BernieSanders.com.

- Are you sick of kooky GOP candidates and Hillary's bank buddies? So am I. That's why I'm voting for Bernie Sanders.

- Aren't you sick and tired of bought and paid for presidential candidates? Bernie Sanders is the only one who isn't. He's the only one who will put the American people first.

- I think it comes down to either voting for a buffoon (Trump), a bank buddy (Clinton), or a Bernie Sanders revolution that puts the needs of the 99% above those of the 1%.

- Oh, come on, admit it: You like socialism. You like Social Security, Medicare, fire departments, a socialized postal system, and public education. Bernie Sanders hears you. He wants to do more of those things.

- Aren't you getting sick and tired of hearing about people in other countries enjoying free universal healthcare and free college? Why can't we have that? Isn't this supposed to be the greatest country in the world?

- Bernie Sanders is the only candidate not bought and paid for by big business. The only one who will work for you!

- Bernie's honest. He's consistent. He's experienced. He has more integrity in his little finger than all the other candidates put together. He gets things done. To me, it's Bernie Sanders … or nothing.

- Bernie Sanders is in it to win it. He is in it for us. BernieSanders.com

- You see the mess George W. Bush made, between his one and a half trillion dollar deficit, a falling stock market, and a pathetic record on job creation. And now you want another Republican? *Seriously?*

- If you're rooting for Hillary or any of the Republican candidates, it probably means that you really like it when presidents have strong ties to big banks, big pharma, and big business.

- From my perspective, it's Bernie Sanders, or more of that "trickle up" economy that the GOP and Hillary love so much.

- Do you seriously think there is one GOP candidate fit to lead this country?

- You say you hate war. You hate unemployment. You hate budget deficits. You hate corporate greed. But you vote Republican. I'm confused.

- Admit it: Doesn't it irritate you that people in other countries have free universal healthcare and free public college tuition? Well, it irritates me!

- One of my favorite Bernie Sanders quotes is: "No one who works forty hours a week should be living in poverty."

- Given his experience, integrity, wisdom, and commitment to the American people, I think Bernie Sanders could wind up being our greatest president in a long, long time.

You get the idea. The important thing is to just spread the word, spread the excitement, plant dreams and seeds of hope into the minds of as many people as you can. History will thank you very soon. Don't forget to visit www.berniesanders.com/issues for much, much more information that will not only fill your brain with even more facts, figures, and talking points to share with others, but it will very likely inspire you even more than you already are.

The Revolution Thing

Revolution (rev-uh-loo-shun) noun: Activity or movement designed to effect fundamental changes in the socioeconomic situation.
Merriam Webster Dictionary

You say you want a revolution? Apparently, you are not alone. With the soon-to-be-realized landslide victory of Bernie Sanders nearly upon us, 2016 is destined to be remembered as a truly historic year. But history will not be made merely because America was finally, after so many years, given the opportunity to elect a president who was truly "by the people and for the people," or because America actually stood up, cried out, and seized that opportunity. History will be made, most of all, because of what this election *means*.

2016 is slated to be remembered as the year during which a peaceful *revolution* took place on American soil. This is not a mere "shake-up." It is not a "movement" such as the Free Speech movement or the Pro Life movement. No, we are not talking about a level of change that affects life on a specific level or affects only a certain group of people. This is far bigger, broader, and deeper than that. Indeed, 2016 is on-track to become one of those truly historic Zeitgeist-altering years: a year when America started over and began to remake itself on an absolutely fundamental level.

And this revolution will not end with the election of a revolutionary figure like Bernie Sanders, nor with the changes he will be bringing to Washington and to the American people. As is most often the case with revolutions, ours represents a beginning, not an end.

No, once America has its first taste of government for the people, healthcare without financial hardship or ruin, college without indenture, and full-time employment without food stamps, there will be no turning back. Life will change, but for the better. It will be better for all of us – even for the 1% (as we will see in a moment). Life will change dramatically and the progressive, forward-motion exhilaration of living a better life will succumb to its own inertia and remain forward moving for a long, long time.

No, there will be no going back. The inequitable "trickle up" system will not be allowed back into our socio-economic paradigm. And this new and improved life of ours will *not* be covertly snatched away by big money a second time. American will be wise to any such a move from now on.

Fool me once ... shame on you.

Fool me twice ... ain't gonna happen.

One challenge we face is a matter of *framing*; a matter of connotation. To many, the term "revolution" is understandably off-putting. It's scary. After hearing throughout our lives about violent coup d'états in some God-forsaken Latin American jungle nation, or even the constructive but nonetheless bloody overthrow of the communist regimes in Eastern Europe during the late 80s, we want nothing to do with anything even resembling a revolution. Even our own celebrated American Revolution was surely not a fun time to be alive in America, positive outcome or not; well-justified or not.

Indeed, who wouldn't be terrified by the possibility of another revolution? Revolutions can, indeed, be bloody and downright nasty. At the very least, anything messy on a national scale is sure to wreak havoc upon our perhaps comfortable, or at least familiar, lives.

Well, of course. Nobody wants that. But that is only one definition of the term. As stated at the beginning of this chapter, one definition for revolution, as offered by Merriam-Webster, is this: "Activity or movement designed to effect fundamental changes in the socioeconomic situation."

It's a lot like water. You can sustain life with it … or you can end life with it. It's all in how you use it. Revolution, in its purest and most peaceful form is *not* to be feared and not to be abhorred. It is not messy. And it is all good.

No, revolution is simply change on a broad scale. In the case of the Bernie Sanders revolution, it is simply change for the better, as in, better lives, and on a very broad scale, as in, three hundred nineteen million Americans. It is change won through well-intentioned voting for a well-intentioned man wielding no weapon other than the conviction and desire to help the American people secure a better life.

That is all.

And that, make no mistake, is much.

The revolution of this day, in these United States, is one of peace. It is one of prosperity: prosperity for the working people of America – the people who work to make America work. It is one of fairness: one that offers, at the very least, an opportunity for all Americans who are willing to work to actually live the American dream; to live without poverty or unfair struggle, to participate in our economy, to share in our pursuit of happiness. It is one of betterment: a better version of America – strong, yes, but also a place where three hundred nineteen million people can say "I like living here. Life in America is good."

So, you say you want a revolution? Fabulous. Now go out and make one. Make it a good one. Do all that you can to help Bernie Sanders make it to the White House, first by your vision, second by your action, third by your vote.

And we will all be the better for it – even the 1%. Even they stand to benefit from and enjoy the fruits of a Bernie Sanders presidency and the revolution to which it belongs. They just don't know it yet. But why shouldn't they stand to benefit? Like most working Americans, they have children, too. Of course they want their children to be happy. Certainly they want their children to live in a nation and a world with fewer wars. Naturally they want their children to live their lives in a world not ravaged by climate change and its resulting droughts, instability, and terrorism.

They, the 1%, absolutely love their children. Of course they want them to live in a country they can be proud of, a country that does right for its citizens, a country made safer not by the construction of more prisons, but by the lessening of poverty. They want their children to live in a nation not feared or abhorred by the rest of the world, but revered and admired by the rest of the world. A country that is, once again, the envy of the world. A country that is great, not greedy. A country onto which the promise of prosperity has truly trickled down for everyone to enjoy – and one which has the universal happiness to prove it.

Who, in the name of God, wouldn't want that?

Our country stands to gain so much from our efforts to help elect Bernie Sanders as our 45th president. We are many millions strong. The months that lie before us will show the world just how strong we are.

Stan Munslow

About the Author

Stan Munslow is an author and educator with a passion for all things political and an obsession with what is *right*. He lives in Coventry, Rhode Island with his wife and almost-human Maltese, "Boo." He is also the father of three bright and beautiful teenage daughters who he wants beyond all else to inherit a word that is good, kind, and the best that it can be.